CW01213061

Original title:
After the Rain

Copyright © 2024 Swan Charm
All rights reserved.

Author: Kene Elistrand
ISBN HARDBACK: 978-9916-89-664-8
ISBN PAPERBACK: 978-9916-89-665-5
ISBN EBOOK: 978-9916-89-666-2

The Color of Reassurance

In hues of warmth, the sun does rise,
Whispers of comfort in the skies.
Gentle hands in twilight's grace,
Coloring hearts, a soft embrace.

With every shade, a promise made,
In laughter's shade, our fears do fade.
A canvas bright, our spirits lift,
In every stroke, a cherished gift.

Beneath the Silvered Glow

Moonlight dances on the stream,
Casting shadows, weaving dreams.
In silver beams, the night unfolds,
Stories whispered, secrets told.

Calm envelops the quiet air,
Peaceful moments, free from care.
Nature's sigh, a sweet refrain,
Beneath the glow, all fears wane.

Mosaic of New Growth

Tiny sprouts push through the ground,
In vibrant colors, life is found.
A patchwork quilt of earth and sky,
Rebirth in every leaf held high.

Wonders bloom with each embrace,
In every corner, hope finds space.
Nature weaves a tale so grand,
Mosaic made by unseen hands.

Soft Exhalation of the Earth

In morning's hush, the world awakes,
With gentle sighs, the silence breaks.
The earth breathes deep, a tender song,
In harmony where we belong.

Roots entwine in rich embrace,
Nature's pulse, a steady pace.
Softly cradled in her care,
Life's exhalation fills the air.

Glasgow's Cleansing Ritual

Rain falls softly on the street,
Whispers of life in every beat.
Cobblestones glisten, stories unfold,
A city's heart warmed, brave and bold.

Pigeons dance in the misty air,
While locals bustle without a care.
Each droplet tells of journeys past,
In Glasgow's embrace, shadows cast.

Artisans weave in colors bright,
Mending fabrics under gray light.
Graffiti blooms where hope ignites,
Cleansing spirits through the nights.

Voices rise in joyful song,
Together they thrive, where we belong.
Through rain and storm, they stand as one,
Glasgow's tale has just begun.

Beneath the grey, the sky is wide,
Where dreams awaken, visions bide.
In every corner, tales do spin,
A cleansing ritual, life begins.

Beneath the Rainbow's Shadow

Beneath the arc of colors bright,
Shadows linger, hidden from sight.
A world unfolds in gentle grace,
Each hue a memory, time won't erase.

Children laugh in the cool spring rain,
Finding joy in a sweet refrain.
While skies weep, a promise shines,
Hope awakens in tangled vines.

From dark to light, the journey flows,
In every heart, a secret glows.
Even storms can bring us peace,
In quiet moments, fears release.

The earth absorbs the falling tears,
Washing away the weight of fears.
Beneath that arch, life finds its way,
In vibrant colors, come what may.

We dance in puddles, laughter free,
Stories spun 'neath the grand marquee.
Life's blessing rained from above,
Under the shadow, we grow in love.

Hope Sprouts in the Wet Soil

In the dampness where green thrives,
Life emerges, and beauty strives.
Each seedling pushes through the ground,
In soft whispers, new dreams abound.

Wet soil cradles tender shoots,
Nature's nurture, life in roots.
Raindrops kiss the earth with grace,
Fostering growth in this sacred space.

Hope unfurls in every leaf,
Reaching for sun, shedding grief.
A vibrant tapestry begins,
As life's symphony softly spins.

In the silence, strength is born,
Each dawn greets a new uniform.
For through the struggle and the strife,
Sprouts arise, breathing with life.

Nature whispers, 'Hold on tight,'
Every petal adds to the light.
In the wet soil where dreams are sown,
Hope takes root, and we are never alone.

The Resilient Bloom

Through cracks in concrete, beauty fights,
A bloom emerges, chasing light.
Against the odds, it finds its place,
In a world that can seem a race.

Petals stretch in vibrant hue,
Painting the gray with hope anew.
Every breeze a gentle touch,
In stillness, it learns to trust much.

Roots dig deep in barren land,
Clinging to earth, a firm stand.
Each droplet nourishes the dream,
In unity, they rise and gleam.

Seasons shift, yet still it grows,
In winter's chill, the spirit knows.
In rain and sun, through joy and gloom,
A testament to life's own bloom.

Resilient hearts, like flowers strong,
Together we weave a timeless song.
With colors bold, we shall prevail,
For in our strength, all spirits sail.

Ephemeral Raindrop Dreams

In the hush of the night,
Raindrops kiss the ground,
Whispers of fleeting time,
Silent dreams abound.

Drifting on the breeze,
Softly they will fade,
A dance of memories,
In twilight's cascade.

Each drop a secret spun,
A brief tale to tell,
In the arms of the sky,
Where shadows dwell.

Wrapped in silver light,
Moments lost in flight,
Ephemeral wonders,
Glittering, then slight.

As dawn breaks anew,
With sun's gentle gleam,
Raindrops hide away,
But linger in dreams.

The Breath of Revival

Emerging from the quiet,
Spring whispers its call,
Nature takes a breath,
Revival for us all.

A blossom unfolds,
Petals drink the light,
Colors burst anew,
In a vibrant flight.

The streams start to flow,
Chasing winter's grip,
With each drop of rain,
Life's gentle sip.

In the warmth of sun,
Character returns,
With a heart so bold,
The spirit yearns.

As blooms paint the world,
Hope's canvas ignites,
The breath of revival,
Through days and nights.

Glimmers on the Pavement

After the rain's soft touch,
Pavement gleams and shines,
Mirrored dreams below,
In silvered designs.

Streetlights flicker softly,
Casting golden globes,
Footsteps echo lightly,
In their cozy robes.

Shadows waltz in pairs,
As the twilight glows,
Each glimmer a whisper,
In evening's prose.

Memories arise,
Beneath the soft beams,
In every deep puddle,
Lay lost hopes and dreams.

Together we move,
On paths of light and shade,
In this dance of life,
Each moment, portrayed.

Rebirth in Petals

In the garden of souls,
Petals gently spread,
A tapestry of life,
Where all hope is fed.

Buds begin to open,
A chorus of hues,
Spring's vibrant embrace,
In morning's soft dew.

Winds carry the scent,
Of fresh blooms in air,
Nature's sweet reminder,
Of love everywhere.

From ashes we rise,
With each bloom reborn,
In cycles of life,
Every heart worn.

Rebirth in petals,
Whispers soft and true,
In the arms of the earth,
All begins anew.

Glittering Paths of Renewal

Beneath the stars, where dreams ignite,
New journeys form in the silent night.
Whispers of hope in the cool, fresh air,
Each step we take, leads us somewhere rare.

Fields of flowers, colors so bright,
Guide us gently, with pure delight.
Nature's canvas, vibrant and wide,
Holds the secrets where joys abide.

Winds of change, they softly call,
Encouraging us to rise, not fall.
With open hearts and courage bold,
We trace new paths, where dreams unfold.

In every challenge, a spark of grace,
With every moment, we find our place.
Embracing the journey, come what may,
Together, we shine, lighting the way.

So let us dance on this path anew,
With laughter and love as our guiding hue.
In unity, we'll find our way,
Glittering paths, where hopes will stay.

The Softness of a Wet Palette

A canvas waits, drenched in hues,
Whispers of color, soft and true.
Each brush stroke tells a tender tale,
In droplets of paint, we set our sail.

Lush greens mingle with deep ocean blue,
The sky's warm blush, kissed by morning dew.
With every blend, emotions collide,
In the softness, our dreams abide.

Swirls of crimson, passion ignites,
Where shadows dance in soft moonlight.
Wet palettes breathe with each gentle touch,
Every layer speaks, reveals so much.

As colors merge, new worlds unfurl,
Creating peace in this vibrant swirl.
Through artistry, our hearts unite,
In the wetness, we find our light.

So let the colors play and intertwine,
The softness speaks, a language divine.
In every palette, joy we find,
With strokes of love, our spirits aligned.

Rebirth in Every Drop

Rain falls softly on thirsty ground,
In every drop, new life is found.
Awakening seeds long held in sleep,
Nature's promise, a secret to keep.

With each gentle touch from the sky,
The world transforms, whispers a sigh.
The earth drinks deep, absorbing each gem,
Rebirth begins, as life finds its stem.

Colors burst forth, bright and alive,
In droplets' dance, all creatures thrive.
A melody sung by leaves in the breeze,
In the rhythm of rain, all hearts find ease.

Awakening dreams in the cool morning mist,
Every moment, nature's perfect tryst.
Together, we bloom, like flowers in spring,
In the heart of the storm, our spirits take wing.

So embrace the rain, the gift from above,
In every drop, there's a promise of love.
For life is a cycle, ever so deep,
In the heart of the rain, our dreams we keep.

Shimmering Threads of Light

Woven through moments, fragile yet bright,
Shimmering threads dance in the light.
Glistening strands of all that we are,
Connecting our souls, like each shining star.

In twilight's embrace, where day meets night,
We find the beauty in shadows' flight.
Each thread a story, whispered and spun,
Tales of struggle, hope, and fun.

Through valleys of doubt and mountains of dreams,
The threads entwine, creating our seams.
With every heartbeat, a tale to share,
In the web of existence, we weave with care.

Illuminated paths where we once felt lost,
Now shimmer with promise, no matter the cost.
With courage, we follow the paths we create,
In the light of connection, we celebrate fate.

So hold onto those threads, both gentle and bright,
For in every weave, shines our collective light.
Together we flourish, our spirits entwined,
In the shimmering threads, true love we find.

Secrets Held in Damp Soil

Whispers linger near roots,
Hidden tales of the earth,
Ancient dreams softly bloom,
Nurtured by silent mirth.

Life curls in a dark embrace,
Under leaves, shadows play,
Buried treasures call our name,
Resting in soil's ballet.

Fingers scrape the cool ground,
Unraveling secrets deep,
Each layer a story told,
Awakening dreams from sleep.

In the stillness, time slows,
Nature's heart beats within,
Life pulses through damp earth,
Where all beginnings begin.

From the soil, we emerge,
Carrying whispers of lore,
Secrets held in damp soil,
A dance forevermore.

Murmurs Beneath Cloudy Canopies

Above, the sky grows gray,
Whispers float on the breeze,
Leaves rustle in the thought,
Nature's voice through the trees.

Shadows blend in the light,
Echoing stories untold,
Where dreams intertwine softly,
Within the forest so bold.

Murmurs weave through the air,
Secrets shared with the moss,
Every branch holds a tale,
Every leaf knows the cost.

Clouds drift, a curtain drawn,
Silence drapes, thick and still,
In the dark, voices rise,
An orchestra of goodwill.

Beneath canopies wide,
Magic dances in flight,
Hushed tones brush the branches,
Carrying dreams through the night.

Laughter Between the Drips

Pitter-patter, a soft rain,
Laughter bounces on stones,
Echoes blend with the drops,
Filling the world with tones.

Between each splash, we meet,
Smiles glimmer in the mist,
Every droplet a secret,
Every giggle, a twist.

Nature's chorus sings loud,
As puddles mirror our glee,
Dancing feet find their rhythm,
In the rain's jubilee.

Wet grass whispers our names,
While the sky, gray and bright,
Shares moments of pure joy,
Wrapped in warmth, out of sight.

In this playful embrace,
Our hearts jump to the beat,
Laughter mingles with raindrops,
Magic found in the street.

Underneath a Shimmering Veil

Stars twinkle like secrets,
Whispers of night draw near,
Draped in a silken sheet,
The darkness holds its dear.

Veils of silver and gray,
Float gently on the air,
Dreams shimmer in the night,
Caught in time, unaware.

Softness wraps the still world,
As shadows bow and sway,
Mysteries wait to unfold,
Underneath where hearts play.

Beneath this starry dome,
Echoes of love take flight,
Boundless, we seek the glow,
Guided by passion's light.

In twilight's gentle arms,
Life pulses, tender and real,
Underneath a shimmering veil,
Truth awaits, soft to feel.

The Last Thrum of Thunder

Dark clouds gather, heavy and low,
Lightning dances, the winds start to blow.
A rumble echoes, deep in the night,
The storm whispers secrets, hidden from sight.

Raindrops fall, stitching the sky,
As nature's symphony begins to cry.
Once fierce and wild, now soft and sweet,
The earth drinks deeply, a tranquil retreat.

Cumulus shadows drift far away,
The sun peeks out, ending the fray.
A gentle hush, the storm bids farewell,
In the calm that follows, a tale to tell.

With every thrum, the heart beats true,
Remnants of thunder, a memory's cue.
As night falls softly, stars take their place,
In the silence left, find your grace.

The last thrum fades, but leaves its mark,
An echoing song, a love in the dark.
Hold it close, this fleeting sound,
For in the quiet, beauty is found.

Awakened Colors

Morning breaks, colors unfold,
Whispers of beauty, stories untold.
Petals unfurl in the warm sunlight,
Every hue dances, vivid and bright.

Crimson and gold, a vibrant blend,
Nature's palette, beginning and end.
The grass glistens, kissed by the dew,
Each shade a promise, fresh and new.

Birds flit and flutter, a joyous tune,
Painting the sky beneath the moon.
The world awakens, life in a rush,
Colors collide in a joyful hush.

In gardens where dreams begin to bloom,
Awakened colors push back the gloom.
Every glance holds a spark of delight,
A reminder that beauty's in sight.

So let your heart be touched by this scene,
Awakened colors where life has been.
For every moment, both near and far,
Reflects the wonder, like a shining star.

Wildflowers in the Wake

Upon the hill where silence lies,
Wildflowers bloom, reaching for the skies.
In hues of gold and shades of blue,
They whisper secrets of the morning dew.

Gentle breezes carry sweet perfume,
A symphony played in nature's room.
Each petal dances, a story unfolds,
Of sunlit adventures and treasures untold.

In the meadow's heart, they sway and twirl,
Among the grass, each blossom a pearl.
Together they flourish, wild and free,
A tapestry woven as far as the eye can see.

Yet storms may pass, and shadows may fall,
But wildflowers rise, defying it all.
Through all the trials, they hold their grace,
A reminder of beauty in every place.

So walk where they flourish, breathe in their cheer,
For wildflowers speak, when hearts choose to hear.
In their gentle presence, find joy on the rise,
As life's fleeting moments bloom before your eyes.

Rainbows in the Mist

After the rain, the world feels anew,
A canvas of colors, bathed in dew.
Through wisps of mist, a vision so bright,
A rainbow emerges, casting pure light.

Softly it arches, a bridge in the air,
Linking the heavens with Earth, everywhere.
Each color tells tales of wonder and love,
Whispers of magic from skies up above.

Beneath the horizon, dreams start to bloom,
Chasing away shadows, dispelling the gloom.
With every glance, hope paints the scene,
A promise of joy, forever serene.

In moments of doubt, when storms come to play,
Remember the rainbows, they're never far away.
Embrace the colors, let your spirit soar,
For after the rain, there's always more.

So wander with wonder, through mist and through light,
And seek out those rainbows, brilliant and bright.
In the heart of the storm, watch the beauty twist,
And find your own path through the soft, swirling mist.

A Symphony of New Beginnings

In dawn's soft glow, we rise anew,
The whispers of hope, a gentle cue.
Each heartbeat sings a vibrant song,
A canvas fresh, where dreams belong.

With every step, the past we shed,
Embracing paths where futures thread.
A dance of life through trials faced,
In every moment, love is laced.

The air is filled with fragrant cheer,
As sunlight breaks, dissolving fear.
Together we stand, hand in hand,
Building the dreams we have planned.

With vibrant hues, the world awakes,
In harmony, our spirit quakes.
The symphony swells, a joyous sound,
A journey new, where hope is found.

Let laughter ring and voices blend,
In this grand tale, we will transcend.
For every end is just the start,
A symphony played from the heart.

Nature's Tender Embrace

A rustling leaf in gentle breeze,
The chirping birds sing melodies.
Each petal soft, a vibrant hue,
In nature's arms, our spirits grew.

The bubbling brook, a soothing sound,
Where peace and quiet can be found.
Beneath the boughs, we seek our rest,
In every corner, nature's best.

A blanket of stars in night's embrace,
The moonlight paints a silver trace.
With every breath, a gift so pure,
In this wild land, our hearts endure.

The mountains rise, strong and tall,
With whispers soft, they beckon all.
Each dawn brings colors, fresh and grand,
In nature's touch, we understand.

Through fields of gold and skies of blue,
The world around us feels so true.
In this lush realm, we find our place,
Forever held in nature's grace.

Drenched Serenity

Raindrops fall with rhythmic grace,
Each one a kiss on nature's face.
Moments still, as time stands still,
A symphony played from the hill.

The world glistens, a polished gem,
Reflection deep, a peaceful hymn.
With every drop, the soil drinks deep,
Awakening dreams from slumber's sleep.

In puddles form, the sky mirrored,
Chaos fades, the heart is stirred.
With soothing sounds, the storm aligns,
In drenched serenity, joy entwines.

Clouds release their heavy weight,
Renewed, the earth, a moment late.
The air, so fresh, a fragrant blend,
In nature's cleanse, our worries mend.

As daylight breaks, the rain may cease,
The world transformed, a newfound peace.
In silence sweet, we breathe, we sigh,
In drenched serenity, spirits fly.

When Light Returns to the World

In shadowed moments, hope grows dim,
Yet deep within, our spirits brim.
A flicker bright, a guiding star,
When light breaks through, it heals the scar.

The dawn unfolds, a golden ray,
Chasing the night, it lights the way.
With every hue, our hearts ignite,
When light returns, we find our fight.

In tangled paths where fears reside,
The warmth of sun will be our guide.
With every step, the dark recedes,
When light returns, it plants new seeds.

So take a breath, let shadows fade,
In blossomed dreams, our hopes invade.
The world aglow, a vibrant swirl,
When light returns to all the world.

Together we rise, hand in hand,
To chase the darkness from this land.
In every heartbeat, love's refrain,
When light returns, we break the chain.

When the Storm Fades

Dark clouds retreat, the sky turns clear,
Soft light breaks through, it draws us near.
Puddles reflect, a world washed anew,
Whispers of peace in the gentle hue.

Raindrops decrease, a fading sound,
Nature exhales, beauty unbound.
Hope springs eternal, as colors collide,
In silence we stand, where chaos has tried.

Nature's Cleansing Breath

Mountains breathe deep, swallowing the mist,
Trees sway in rhythm, in nature's twist.
Rivers flow freely, carving the land,
Each drop a promise, a future so grand.

Morning dew glistens, a sparkling dress,
The world awakes in tranquil finesse.
Air sweetens lightly, fills lungs with grace,
In every pause, we find our place.

Liquid Crystals on Leaves

Morning sun kisses, the emerald sheen,
Liquid crystals dance, a vibrant scene.
Nature's jewels catch the light so bright,
Each droplet tells tales of day and night.

Gentle winds carry whispers of peace,
Leaves shimmer softly, as worries release.
Autumn's embrace paints colors that blend,
In every reflection, a moment to tend.

Echoes of a Watery Dance

Ripples tease softly, a rhythmic embrace,
Water's sweet laughter highlights the space.
Frogs croak their song, a chorus in play,
Nature unites in a wondrous ballet.

Moonlight then glimmers, on surfaces clear,
All beings listen, as night draws near.
In the stillness, we find our own part,
Echoes of water stir deep in the heart.

Whispers of a Fresh Dawn

Morning light begins to break,
Softly kissed by night's retreat.
Birds sing sweetly, hopes awake,
Life renewed beneath our feet.

Gentle breezes start to flow,
Carrying scents of the bloom.
Colors dance in vibrant show,
Chasing away shadows' gloom.

A world reborn in golden hues,
Promises whisper in the air.
Each moment, a chance to choose,
To honor dreams and dare.

Sunbeams play on dewy grass,
Nature's canvas, fresh and bright.
Time moves slowly, seconds pass,
In the magic of the light.

So let us breathe this dawn in deep,
And take its blessings, bold and free.
For in its whispers, secrets seep,
Awakening the soul to be.

Beneath the Cleansing Sky

Raindrops fall like whispered dreams,
Cleansing earth with gentle hands.
Each droplet sparkles, softly gleams,
Nourishing the thirsting lands.

Clouds roll in with moody grace,
Dancing lightly on the breeze.
Nature's tears, a sweet embrace,
Bringing life with such ease.

Puddles form like mirrors fair,
Reflecting worlds in muted tones.
In this stillness, time lays bare,
A symphony of nature's moans.

Thunder rumbles, lightning strikes,
A chorus loud, yet sweet, it sings.
In the chaos, life ignites,
Renewal comes on powerful wings.

So let the rain fall, clear and bright,
Washing worries from our sight.
Underneath this cleansing sky,
We find hope as we learn to fly.

The Earth Shimmers Again

As the sun dips low and glows,
Golden rays begin to play.
Shadows stretch while twilight flows,
Night approaches, ending day.

Fields aglow in amber light,
Every blade of grass awakes.
Nature breathes in pure delight,
In the dance that daylight makes.

Stars emerge, the sky adorned,
Whispers of the night take hold.
In this silence, dreams are born,
Stories woven, brave and bold.

The moonrise glistens on the stream,
A silver path that beckons close.
In its glow, reality seems
To settle into calm repose.

When tomorrow brings the dawn,
The earth will shimmer, love renewed.
In cycles of the night and morn,
Life's beauty will be shown, ensued.

Reflections in Puddles

After rain, the world transformed,
Puddles form like glassy eyes.
Sky and earth in water warmed,
Mirrored dreams beneath the skies.

Colors bleed and softly swirl,
A palette rich, a canvas bare.
In each ripple, stories twirl,
Echoes of the love we share.

Children jump with laughter bright,
Splashing through the glistening sheen.
Joy reflected, pure delight,
In these moments, we have seen.

Holding storms within their frame,
Each puddle tells a tale unique.
Beneath the drumming, all the same,
A quiet strength in watery peak.

So pause awhile, reflect and gaze,
At fleeting moments caught anew.
In puddles' depth, our spirits blaze,
A world of wonder, fresh with hue.

Creation's Reset Button

In the hush of dawn's embrace,
Whispers of a world anew,
Stars fade into the brightening sky,
Nature's breath, a gentle cue.

Rivers start to hum their song,
Mountains stand with heads held high,
Each leaf dances to its beat,
As if to bid the night goodbye.

Winds carry tales of old,
Seeds awaken, dreams unfold,
Eager blooms rise from the earth,
A symphony of life, retold.

With every drop of morning dew,
The canvas wakes, vividly bright,
Colors burst in joyful cheer,
Creation loves its own delight.

Hope cascades like morning light,
Renewal paints each dawn anew,
In the stillness, find your heart,
As life's masterpiece comes into view.

Serenity in the Remains

Amidst the ruins of the past,
Silence settles soft and deep,
Echoes of what once stood tall,
In crumbling walls, the memories sleep.

Nature weaves through broken stone,
Creeping vines in earnest grace,
Flowers bloom where shadows lay,
Finding peace in every space.

Time holds secrets in its palm,
Gently sifting through the days,
Whispers beckon from the ground,
In twilight's glow, the heart stays.

Ghosts of laughter fill the air,
Each heartbeat ties the past to now,
Moments captured in the dust,
In silence, we still make a vow.

In memories sewn with thread of gold,
Existence glows, fragile yet bold,
Find serenity in what remains,
A quiet tale of love retold.

The Return of the Rainbow's Bow

After the rain, the sky breaks free,
Colors dance in vibrant arcs,
Nature's brush paints vivid dreams,
Bringing warmth to chilly parks.

Each hue whispers a sweet refrain,
Red for passion, blue for peace,
Golden rays from the sun's embrace,
In harmony, all sorrows cease.

Children laugh beneath the glow,
Pointing fingers to the heights,
Chasing shadows in the sun,
Where magic weaves its simple sights.

The bow reminds us, hope remains,
Even through storms that make us bend,
In every drop, a promise claims,
That beauty waits, around each bend.

So here we stand, hearts open wide,
To greet the colors as they blend,
In unity, we find our path,
With love, we rise, and fears we mend.

Laughter in Crystal Beads

In every bead, a story told,
Twinkling tales of moments shared,
Joy captured in a child's smile,
Fragments of love, gently spared.

As sunlight dances on the glass,
Colors burst, like laughter's sound,
Each shimmer weaves a timeless thread,
Connecting hearts in circles round.

With every clasp, a memory sealed,
A journey made from hand to heart,
Together, smiles shine bright and clear,
For laughter is the truest art.

Worn on wrists or around the neck,
Crystal beads hum a lively tune,
Echoing laughter's sweetest notes,
Under the watchful gaze of the moon.

So let us string our joys and dreams,
In jewelry of memories bright,
For laughter, like these crystal beads,
Is the treasure that brings pure light.

Curls of Mist in the Air

Curls of mist weave through the trees,
Whispers of secrets, a soothing breeze.
Veils of gray dance with the dawn,
Nature's brisk breath, a delicate yawn.

Footsteps soft on a carpet of dew,
Every moment feels fresh and new.
The world awakens, a canvas unspun,
In the morning light, a day to be won.

The sun peeks through the veil of the night,
Casting shadows, with warmth it ignites.
Curls of mist gently fade away,
As bright colors bloom in the heart of the day.

Time drifts slowly, as if in a dream,
With every heartbeat, we flow like a stream.
Embracing the morn, with its tender charm,
Curls of mist bring solace, they soothe and disarm.

Hope Pours from the Clouds

Dark skies loom, but don't lose sight,
Hope pours down, in glimmers of light.
Raindrops carry dreams from above,
Each one whispers tales of love.

Fields drink deeply, thirst quenched anew,
Life emerges in vibrant hues.
Colors blossom, seeds start to sprout,
In the heart of shadows, there's no room for doubt.

Clouds release their burdens with grace,
Washing the world, leaving a trace.
Footprints of puddles, bright and round,
Echoing laughter, a joyous sound.

With every drop, the heart learns to sing,
A melody soft, that hope always brings.
So let the rains come, and spirits rise,
For in every storm, the sun also flies.

Graced by Gentle Tears

Graced by gentle tears, the moonlight weeps,
Kissing the earth, where solace keeps.
Stars twinkle softly in the night sky,
Listening to dreams, as they drift and fly.

Reflections shimmer in pools of gold,
Stories untold in the silence unfold.
Each tear that falls brings cleansing release,
In the deep shadows, we find our peace.

The heart opens wide to the world's tender sigh,
Embracing the moments as they flutter by.
In the gentle rain, there's beauty to find,
A celebration of love and the ties that bind.

Graced by gentle tears, we grow and mend,
Hearts carved in time, where sorrows blend.
Let the tears fall, let the stories flow,
In the quiet night, our spirits will glow.

The Pitcher of Renewal

The pitcher stands, a beacon of hope,
Filled with dreams, helping us cope.
Pouring forth a fountain of light,
Quenching our thirst, igniting the night.

Filling our hearts with whispers so sweet,
Each drop a promise, our lives to complete.
Under the stars, we gather round,
In the treasure of moments, true joy is found.

The pitcher overflows with laughter and grace,
Carving out memories, time can't erase.
In simple gestures, we find delight,
As the world awakens in soft morning light.

Every sip taken, a moment to share,
The essence of love woven in air.
A pitcher of renewal, forever will flow,
Reviving our spirits, as we bask in its glow.

Evergreen Secrets in Dew

Whispers of dawn on emerald blades,
Soft glimmers caught in morning's gaze.
Nature's breath in fragrant air,
Hiding secrets, silent, rare.

Beneath the boughs, a world concealed,
In every droplet, life revealed.
A dance of light, a tranquil sigh,
Where dreams of green and blue do lie.

Ancient roots in soil deep,
Guarding stories, secrets keep.
Lush canopies, a gentle hold,
Embracing tales of life retold.

Morning's grace in each pure drop,
From towering trees to forest floor, stop.
An ode to life, a soft caress,
In every dew, a quiet bless.

Evergreen secrets, timeless and true,
In every leaf, the old and new.
A symphony of nature's grace,
Reflected in this sacred place.

Silver Linings on Parched Streets

Underneath the sun's harsh glare,
Footsteps echo, dreams laid bare.
Dusty paths where shadows play,
Hope emerges in a bright array.

Cracks in concrete tell their tales,
Of storms endured and whispered wails.
Yet in the grime, a shimmer glows,
A whispering promise that life bestows.

Clouds may gather, skies may weep,
Yet silver linings find their leap.
In every storm, a chance to rise,
To see the world through hopeful eyes.

Even parched streets can bring delight,
With glimmers of joy that shine so bright.
In every heart, a place to dream,
Resilience flows, a steady stream.

As daylight fades, the evening hums,
Carrying whispers of hope that come.
Silver linings dance and sway,
Leading us into a brand new day.

Petals Drink the Sky's Tears

In gardens where the wildflowers bloom,
Each petal cradles nature's loom.
Caught within the morning's light,
They drink the sky's tears, pure and bright.

Butterflies flit on gentle breeze,
Amongst the petals, nature frees.
Soft whispers carried on the air,
In every droplet, worlds laid bare.

Colors blend in laughter's song,
As sunlight kisses, where they belong.
Petals open, reaching wide,
Embracing rain, their faithful guide.

In each soft hue, a story flows,
Of summer's kiss and winter's woes.
Together they dance, a wondrous sight,
Where petals drink the sky's delight.

As day turns dusk, they softly sigh,
In twilight's calm, beneath the sky.
Petals dreaming of the dawn,
In nature's rhythm, they are drawn.

A Symphony in the Shadows

In twilight's hush, the shadows creep,
Where secrets linger, softly sweep.
A symphony of silent grace,
In darkness, beauty finds its place.

Murmurs of night in whispers blend,
Melodies where dreams ascend.
Each flicker holds a hidden tale,
In mystery, the stars unveil.

Ghostly figures dance and sway,
Painting stories where they play.
In every corner, echoes sound,
Life's forgotten tales abound.

The moon conducts with silver beams,
Illuminating lost, old dreams.
In shadows deep, whispers ignite,
A symphony, a world of light.

As night unfolds its velvet cloak,
Every sound, a wordless spoke.
In shadows, life begins to grow,
A symphony that all can know.

In Praise of Quiet Moments

In the hush of dawn's sweet breath,
Time whispers softly, a gentle caress.
Each heartbeat lingers, a quiet depth,
  In solitude's arms, we find our rest.

Sunlight creeps through shaded trees,
  With every rustle, secrets unfold.
The world quiets down, a soft tease,
  In these moments, we feel bold.

Birds softly chirp a morning song,
Nature's symphony, the heart's delight.
In stillness, we learn where we belong,
  Finding peace in the fading night.

With a cup of warmth, we sit and sigh,
Embracing the tranquil, the sweet, the rare.
In quiet moments, time lifts us high,
  And burdens vanish in the tender air.

As the sun sets with a glowing hue,
We muse on all that the day bestowed.
In quiet moments, life feels anew,
  With whispered wishes softly flowed.

A Tapestry of Dewy Delights

Morning breaks with a silken glow,
A tapestry woven in delicate strands.
Dewdrops shimmer where soft breezes blow,
Nature's jewels breathe in our hands.

Each blade of grass wears a crystal crown,
Reflecting dawn's warmth, a fleeting kiss.
In this lush world, worries drown,
We savor each moment, a pure bliss.

Petals unfurl, their colors ablaze,
Filled with the promise of joy and cheer.
In dewy splendor, the heart sings praise,
To the wonders of nature, ever near.

Birds flit through branches, in joyous flight,
Sipping the nectar of a brand new day.
In each drop of dew, a spark of light,
Invites us to dance, come what may.

As sunlight bathes the world in gold,
The tapestry glistens, alive and bright.
With dewy delights, our spirits unfold,
In this vibrant dance of morning light.

Canvas of Clouds

Above us lies a canvas vast,
Strokes of white on a blue embrace.
Clouds drift slowly, shadows cast,
A masterpiece in time and space.

Whispers of wind caress the sky,
As sunbeams play in a gentle waltz.
Each cloud a story drifting by,
In nature's realm, no faults or halts.

Colors shift as the day awakes,
Soft pastels blush in morning's glow.
An artist's dream, the heart overtakes,
With each stroke, a new tale to show.

As daylight fades, the hues grow bold,
A tapestry woven in twilight's sigh.
Golden and crimson, a sight to hold,
The canvas transforms as stars reply.

In stillness, let our spirits rise,
Beneath this wondrous, shifting art.
With every glance at the painted skies,
We find a piece of nature's heart.

Transitioning Skies

Daylight whispers its final song,
As twilight paints the world in hues.
In transitions where shadows belong,
The heart finds solace, softly infused.

Stars begin to flicker and play,
In the canvas where dusk takes flight.
As colors blend and fade away,
New dreams awaken in the night.

The horizons blush in shades profound,
A symphony of silence fills the air.
In these moments, beauty is found,
With every glance, we're lost in prayer.

Clouds drift gently, shifting forms,
Carrying whispers of days gone by.
In the dance of light as the world transforms,
We find our place beneath the sky.

Embrace the shifts, the ebb, and flow,
In transitioning skies, life takes its course.
With every sunset, a new dawn will show,
And in this rhythm, we feel the force.

The Heartbeat of Fresh Earth

Beneath the soil, life stirs anew,
Roots intertwine, a dance so true.
Whispers of growth in the cool, damp air,
Nature's rhythm, gentle and rare.

Raindrops fall, a soft embrace,
Nourishing life, a sacred space.
Each pulse of green, a vibrant sound,
The pulse of earth, profound and bound.

Seeds awaken, ambitions rise,
Hope unfurls under open skies.
In silence, dreams begin to bloom,
A future bright dispels the gloom.

From tiny sprouts to towering trees,
Resilience strong, like the ocean's breeze.
Together they thrive, attuned in grace,
The heartbeat of earth in every place.

In harmony's song, life's promise is sewn,
With every heartbeat, we are not alone.
Nature and spirit, together, they play,
Cradling beginnings in a tender sway.

A Serenade to Sunlit Paths

Golden paths where shadows dance,
Each step invites a fleeting chance.
Beams of light through leaves cascade,
Nature's song in sunlight made.

A gentle breeze caresses skin,
Whispers secrets to let them in.
Violet blooms on either side,
Their fragrance and beauty, a joyful guide.

Rustling leaves in playful cheer,
Echoes of laughter fill the air.
Winding trails beneath the sky,
Where dreams take flight and spirits fly.

Sunset paints the horizon wide,
An artist's brush as day subsides.
Memories linger in every hue,
A serenade, a gift anew.

In the twilight, paths softly glow,
Promises linger in the flow.
With each heartbeat, a journey starts,
A serenade that warms the hearts.

Radiance Following the Tumult

Storm clouds gather, shadows loom,
Yet within, there waits a bloom.
Through the chaos, sunlight breaks,
A gentle warmth, the heart awakes.

Raindrops glisten on vibrant leaves,
Whispering tales the soul believes.
After the strife, beauty reveals,
A canvas of hope that softly heals.

Lightning strikes, a contrast bold,
Nature's fury, a story told.
Yet as the tempest fades away,
Radiance lingers, here to stay.

Wind's caress, a soothing balm,
In every heart, a quiet calm.
Resilience born from trials faced,
In radiance, we find our place.

Each dawn brings light to past distress,
With open arms, we feel its bless.
From tumult's grip, we rise and gleam,
In radiance, we dream our dream.

Brightness in Nature's Canvas

Mountains rise like ancient kings,
Wrapped in mist, whispers of springs.
A tapestry woven in vibrant hues,
Nature's palette, forever renews.

Fields of gold in sunlight's embrace,
Where wildflowers bloom with grace.
Colors collide, a joyful cheer,
In the canvas, no room for fear.

Beneath the boughs, shadows waltz,
Each nuance whispers, nature's vaults.
From emerald greens to starlit skies,
In every corner, magic lies.

Rainbows arch from stormy plight,
A promise of peace, a guiding light.
In each scene, a story unfolds,
Timeless tales, like treasures of gold.

With every breath, the colors dance,
Nature invites us to take a chance.
In brightness found, our spirits soar,
On nature's canvas, forever more.

Fleeting Moments of Clarity

In whispers soft, the truth appears,
A glance, a sigh, dissolving fears.
These moments brief, they come and go,
A fleeting spark, a gentle glow.

With every breath, the chaos calms,
Like soothing waves and nature's charms.
In quiet spaces, thoughts align,
We glimpse a peace, a life benign.

The world may swirl in endless haste,
Yet stillness holds a sacred place.
With open hearts, we catch the light,
In fleeting moments, we take flight.

As shadows fade and colors blend,
We find the strength to start again.
Each fleeting chance, we hold it near,
A memory etched, forever clear.

In honesty, our spirits rise,
Through fleeting moments, we become wise.
With every breath, we learn to see,
The clarity in what will be.

Serenity's Drizzle

A gentle rain, a soft embrace,
Each drop a note, a calm replace.
The world awash in silver shades,
Where peace is found, and worry fades.

Beneath the trees, the whispers play,
As nature sings, come what may.
The rhythm of the falling drops,
A lullaby that never stops.

With every splash, the heart unfolds,
In quiet strength, each story told.
A moment shared, beneath the clouds,
In stillness wrapped, away from crowds.

The earth receives its cool caress,
In puddles deep, our thoughts digress.
A tranquil pause, a breath of air,
In serenity's sweet affair.

As twilight casts its final hue,
The drizzles dance, the world anew.
In droplets' touch, we find our place,
Embracing life with gentle grace.

The Taste of Drenched Air

After the storm, the world awakes,
In fragrant notes, the freshness makes.
A breath of life in every sigh,
The taste of rain that kissed the sky.

In stillness deep, the whispers blend,
As nature's voice begins to mend.
Each inhalation, sweet and pure,
The essence of the earth's allure.

With every step on soil renewed,
The summer's song, a heartbeat's mood.
In harmony, the senses dance,
As life unfolds in its expanse.

The amber glow of setting sun,
A citrus kiss, a day well done.
In vibrant hues, the air respects,
A melody that life connects.

As twilight drapes the earth like silk,
We taste the night, so smooth, so milk.
In every breath, a world to share,
The magic of the drenched air.

Dreamscapes Woven in Water

In liquid realms where dreams reside,
Reflections dance, our souls confide.
The ripples play, a tale unwinds,
In waters deep, the heart inclines.

Beneath the surface, visions bloom,
Each thought a petal, breaking gloom.
In currents swift, we lose our fears,
A tapestry of hopes and tears.

The moonlight weaves its silver thread,
In whispers soft, where once we tread.
With every splash, a story grows,
In fluid grace, the river flows.

With open minds, we dive within,
To find the truths that lie akin.
In dreamscapes rich, we find our spark,
Illuminating paths from dark.

Through waking moments, we reflect,
On waters vast, our souls connect.
In every wave, a chance to see,
The dreamscapes hold our history.

The Quiet Brilliance of Dawn

Soft light spills over the hills,
A whisper wakes the sleeping trees.
Colors blend, like gentle thrills,
As daybreak dances on the breeze.

Birds sing sweetly in the air,
A melody that feels so pure.
In silence, beauty finds its flair,
A moment brief, yet meant to cure.

The world, adorned in golden hues,
Embraces hope, a brand new start.
Each shadow lingers, slowly flews,
While dreams awaken in the heart.

With every breath, the dawn unfolds,
A canvas stretched across the sky.
Life's stories, new and yet retold,
In morning's light, we learn to fly.

So pause and revel in this grace,
As quiet brilliance paints our way.
The dawn, a soft and warm embrace,
Calls forth the promise of the day.

Echoing Heartbeats in the Mist

In twilight's grasp, shadows shift,
The fog envelopes every scene.
Whispers blend, like a sacred gift,
Heartbeats thrum where dreams convene.

Misty veils wrap the world in gray,
As secrets drift on the midnight air.
Moments pause, then slip away,
In shimmering silence, soft and rare.

Through the haze, the echoes call,
A symphony of souls entwined.
Each heartbeat loud within us all,
Resonates with love, unconfined.

Faint glimmers of hope start to gleam,
As dawn approaches from afar.
In each breath, a subtle dream,
A promise written in each star.

Together we chase the quiet night,
Finding courage in the mist.
With every pulse, we feel the light,
Echoing heartbeats, too strong to resist.

Life's Glossy Second Act

In twilight's glow, we shed the past,
A gentle shift in the evening air.
With every shadow, new dreams cast,
Life's glossy hues begin to flare.

The stage is set for tales untold,
Where laughter mingles with the sighs.
Painted stories, brave and bold,
Underneath the starlit skies.

Each moment glimmers like a pearl,
In time's embrace, we start anew.
A dance of fate begins to swirl,
With every heartbeat, we break through.

We rise from ashes, learning grace,
In every stumble, strength we gain.
With courage found in this new space,
We write our stories once again.

So here we are, with hearts ablaze,
In life's second act, we dare to dream.
With glossy paths and daring ways,
We flourish in the fading gleam.

Embracing the Afterglow

When day retreats and colors fade,
The afterglow begins its show.
In twilight's arms, the night cascades,
With every star, our spirits grow.

The world is painted soft and warm,
As shadows gather, lingering near.
A tranquil peace begins to swarm,
Embracing hopes, dissolving fear.

The whispers of the day unwind,
In gentle sighs, a lullaby.
We seek the dreams that we can find,
Beneath the vast and open sky.

With every flicker, hearts ignite,
In afterglow, we find our pace.
Together we embrace the night,
Finding solace in this space.

So let us linger, hand in hand,
As day gives way to starlit glow.
In every breath, we understand,
The beauty found in letting go.

Serenity's Embrace

In the hush of twilight glow,
The whispers of the night softly flow.
Stars adorned like dreams we chase,
Wrapped gently in serenity's embrace.

Calm waters mirror the moon's face,
In this stillness, we find our place.
Breath of silence, a soothing balm,
In the heart of night, we feel so calm.

Nature hums a lullaby sweet,
As time slows down, our pulses meet.
With every sigh, a moment's grace,
Sealed forever in serenity's embrace.

Under the vast, celestial dome,
We wander far, we find our home.
Each flicker of light a gentle trace,
Guiding us through serenity's embrace.

As dawn beckons, light breaks free,
Transforming shadows, tenderly.
Yet in our hearts, we store the space,
Forever held in serenity's embrace.

Mended Skies

Beneath the clouds, the sun will rise,
Painting hues in mended skies.
Threads of gold weave through the grey,
Whispering hope for a brand new day.

Birds take flight, a joyful sound,
In the air, new dreams are found.
Each wingbeat, a promise lies,
Dancing softly in mended skies.

The rain has healed, the storm has passed,
Joyful moments, free at last.
In every heart, the spirit flies,
Bathed in light of mended skies.

As shadows fade with warming light,
Laughter echoes, spirits bright.
Hope takes root, and love complies,
Filling the void of mended skies.

Together, we'll rise, hand in hand,
Painting futures, dreams unplanned.
With every sigh and gentle cries,
We build our world of mended skies.

Dance of the Raindrops

Raindrops fall like nature's tears,
Whispering tales of hopes and fears.
They pluck the strings of earth's soft heart,
In a melody, they play their part.

Each droplet twirls with graceful flow,
Kissing petals in the evening glow.
A ballet spun in wild delight,
The dance of raindrops ignites the night.

Puddles glisten under clouded skies,
Reflecting dreams where spirit flies.
Dancing shadows paint the streets,
As laughter echoes in rhythmic beats.

Wind joins in, a gentle twist,
Nature joins the raindrops' tryst.
An orchestra of water and air,
In harmony, they dance with flair.

As storms retreat, the world revived,
Life awakens, joy derived.
In every drop, a spark that tries,
To tell the tale: the dance of raindrops.

The Earth Sighs Fresh

A gentle breeze caresses the land,
Whispers of life, a tender hand.
Leaves rustle softly in tender mesh,
Awakening nature, the earth sighs fresh.

Flowers bloom with colors bright,
In every petal, pure delight.
Roots drink deep from the nourishing flesh,
As in stillness, the earth sighs fresh.

Mountains stand, regal and tall,
Guardians watching over all.
With every echo, every thresh,
The ancient wisdom, the earth sighs fresh.

Rivers flow with stories old,
Carving paths through time untold.
In harmony, life starts to mesh,
Renewed and vibrant, the earth sighs fresh.

When twilight falls, the stars ignite,
Celestial wonders, pure delight.
Embracing night, with every flesh,
In quiet reverie, the earth sighs fresh.

Secrets Hidden in Damp Earth

In shadows deep, where whispers dwell,
The roots entwine, their stories tell.
Beneath the soil, the secrets hide,
In damp embrace, the past abides.

A flicker here, a hidden trace,
Of life once lived, in this still space.
The earth remembers every seed,
Of silent hopes and growing need.

With every rain, the memories swell,
As dampness builds, they weave their spell.
The whispers rise from ancient ground,
In hidden realms, lost things are found.

The mushrooms bloom in twilight's glow,
In secret nooks, where shadows flow.
They gather tales from years gone by,
In silent watch, the earth's soft sigh.

So if you kneel and bend your ear,
To nature's pulse, the secrets clear.
In every drop, a story lies,
In damp earth's heart, where wisdom sighs.

Awakening the Forgotten

In stillness deep, the dreams await,
For time to turn, for hearts to fate.
Forgotten echoes call the day,
To awaken souls lost in dismay.

The morning sun breaks through the haze,
A gentle touch, the world ablaze.
Whispers rise from slumber's chime,
As shadows weave with threads of time.

In every heart, a spark still glows,
As memories beckon, the river flows.
Awakening the dormant seeds,
To bloom anew with vibrant creeds.

Through misty morn and twilight's song,
The past returns; it won't be long.
Each moment shared, a tale retold,
Of whispers soft, and hearts of gold.

So heed the call, and rise above,
Embrace the fate, and share the love.
In every soul, a story waits,
Awakening the forgotten fates.

Traces of the Cleansed Sky

The sky so pure, a canvas bright,
With colors bold, a stunning sight.
Traces left by storms that passed,
In fading hues, the die was cast.

In evening's glow, the clouds disperse,
Revealing peace, the universe.
A breath of wind, a lover's sigh,
In every sweep, the vast blue sky.

Stars twinkle like dandelion seeds,
On gentle nights, the heart concedes.
Each glimmer tells a tale once lost,
In tranquil nights, we count the cost.

The moon ascends, a silver arc,
Guiding dreamers through the dark.
Traces linger in twilight's breath,
In whispered winds, the dance of death.

So look above; embrace the night,
In cleansed skies, find your delight.
For every trace of light we see,
Is nature's way of setting free.

Echoes of Nature's Breaths

In the forest deep, where shadows play,
Nature breathes, both night and day.
The leaves whisper, a gentle tune,
Echoing softly under the moon.

Each rustling branch, a story spun,
In every breeze, the earth's deep fun.
The river flows with ancient grace,
Reflecting time, and nature's face.

With every sigh, the creatures speak,
In silence loud, the strong and weak.
The chorus rises, serene and true,
In every note, the world anew.

Mountains stand tall, in silence reign,
Holding echoes of joy and pain.
In their arms, the whispers sway,
Guiding lost hearts along the way.

So listen close, to nature's call,
In every breath, you'll find it all.
The echoes linger, through time we tread,
In nature's arms, the past is fed.

A Tapestry of Fresh Beginnings

Threads of hope weave through the air,
New dawn beckons with gentle care.
Each moment brims with endless light,
Stars align to banish the night.

Resilience blooms where shadows fall,
In the heart's chamber, courage calls.
A canvas vast, wild and free,
Our dreams dance bright, as they should be.

The past slips softly into the dawn,
With every step, we're reborn.
Whispers of change thread through the breeze,
In the chorus of life, we find our ease.

Hope's colors paint the skies above,
Nature's tapestry speaks of love.
With every heartbeat, we create,
A journey forged, a brand-new fate.

So let us gather, hand in hand,
To build a world, both brave and grand.
In unity, we find our way,
A tapestry of bright new day.

Gentle Rising Steam

In the morning light, soft and clear,
Steam arises, drawing near.
Whispers of warmth in a quiet room,
Filling the air, dispelling gloom.

Curling tendrils, steam takes flight,
Brings a touch of pure delight.
Kettle sings its soothing tune,
Morning's promise, a gift in bloom.

Tasting the warmth in each small sip,
A moment's pause, the heart's sweet trip.
In steam's embrace, we find our peace,
A gentle rising, worries cease.

Through fragrant herbs and citrus zest,
Nature's bounty, we are blessed.
With every breath, the world seems bright,
Gentle steam, a pure delight.

So let us gather, share our dreams,
In the comfort of rising beams.
A simple cup, a treasured plan,
In the steam's dance, we understand.

A Clearer Horizon

Beneath the skies, so vast and wide,
A clearer horizon calls inside.
With every step, the path we see,
The journey unfolds, wild and free.

Mountains rise with courage grand,
Embracing dreams, we'll firmly stand.
Clouds drift softly in the blue,
A canvas painted fresh and true.

With every sunrise, doubts decay,
The future glimmers in bright array.
Casting shadows from yesterday's fears,
Hope's gentle whispers calm our tears.

Together we tread on this bright ground,
With open hearts, our souls unbound.
We reach for the stars, together we climb,
A clearer horizon, where we flow with time.

In the light's embrace, we find our place,
Strength in unity, a warm embrace.
With every heartbeat, we believe,
In the gift of life, we shall achieve.

The Garden's Gratitude

In the garden where blossoms sing,
Nature shares its vibrant spring.
Petals open, colors burst,
In gratitude, the world is immersed.

Bees hum softly, tending each bloom,
Sunlight dances, dispelling gloom.
Roots reach deep, in soil they stay,
Grateful for life in every way.

With every raindrop, blessings fall,
A testament to nature's call.
Fruits of labor, sweet and bright,
Harvest brings joy, pure delight.

Hands in the earth, we nurture and care,
In every moment, love we share.
The garden flourishes in harmony,
Gratitude's song, for all to see.

So let our hearts in this garden grow,
In the dance of life, let kindness flow.
With every season, lessons bloom,
In the garden's heart, there's always room.

The Dusk's Gentle Caress

The sun dips low in vibrant hues,
Whispers of night in gentle muse.
Shadows stretch as light retreats,
Embracing dusk, the heart repeats.

Stars awaken in the sky,
As the day bids sweet goodbye.
A calm embrace, so soft and slow,
Underneath the twilight glow.

Birds sing softly, wrapping time,
In the chill, the air feels prime.
The world transforms in softest tones,
A melody that rumbles and moans.

Branches dance in evening's grace,
Nature's breath, a warm embrace.
Every leaf begins to sway,
As night declares a peaceful stay.

With every heartbeat, love persists,
In dusk's caress, no moment missed.
Where dreams ignite and spirits soar,
The night unfolds, forevermore.

A Freshet of New Life

Morning breaks with gentle light,
Awakening the world so bright.
Colors splash from every side,
Nature's joy cannot be denied.

Blossoms burst in joyous dance,
Flea of spring, a sweet romance.
Life begins, the earth renews,
In every hour, fresh love ensues.

Birdsong lifts with pure delight,
Melodies weaving day and night.
Tiny creatures, quick and spry,
Frolic under the vast sky.

Streams awaken, running free,
Glistening in the sun's decree.
Ripples laugh, and breezes sigh,
As hopes and dreams begin to fly.

In every bud, a story waits,
Tales of life through nature's gates.
We are born from this bright strife,
In the freshness of new life.

Catching Raindrop Memories

Pitter-patter on windowpanes,
A symphony of soft refrains.
Each drop holds a whisper sweet,
Of times and places, lost, discrete.

Umbrellas bloom like flowers bright,
As hearts unfold in silver light.
Footprints dance in puddles deep,
In joyful leaps, memories creep.

The world, refreshed, breathes anew,
Colors vibrant, every hue.
Children laugh in swirling rain,
Chasing dreams free from refrain.

A rainbow arches, bright and bold,
Stories of wonder to unfold.
In every glint, a spark of glee,
Catching memories, wild and free.

Each raindrop brings a moment's grace,
A fleeting glance, a warm embrace.
Under the clouds, life flows and sways,
In raindrop memories, love stays.

Tears of Gratitude Wash Away

Softly falling, gentle streams,
Carrying with them hidden dreams.
In the silence, hearts unfold,
Stories of the brave and bold.

With each tear, a lesson learned,
In sorrow, gratitude is earned.
Washing fears like morning rain,
Bringing solace to the pain.

Every drop a tale to tell,
Of hope that rose from deepest well.
Memories linger, bittersweet,
In every sorrow, love is meet.

Embracing feelings, pure and raw,
Finding strength within the flaw.
A river flows of past and now,
In heartfelt moments, we avow.

So let the tears cascade and play,
For gratitude will light the way.
Through the storm, we rise anew,
In tears of joy, our spirits grew.

A Glimpse Through the Mist

A shroud of gray enfolds the vale,
Whispers of dawn begin to pale.
Shadows dance in silence deep,
Secrets that the night will keep.

Through the fog, a vision stirs,
Nature's song in sleepy blurs.
Softly waking with each breath,
Awakening life from its death.

Fleeting forms flicker and fade,
In the stillness, peace is made.
A glimpse of light breaks through the haze,
Promising warmth of sunlit days.

The world unravels, colors bloom,
Past the mist, there's room for loom.
Threads of life weave rich and tight,
Transforming shadows into light.

In the quiet, hope takes flight,
Guided by the emerging light.
A glimpse of dawn, a tender kiss,
In shadows, we find our bliss.

Euphony of the Renewed

A symphony, the earth's refrain,
Melodies of loss and gain.
Every note is soft and clear,
Echoes of the life we cheer.

Nature hums a sweet surprise,
Solace found in open skies.
Harmony in every hue,
Life rejoices, born anew.

The rustling leaves, a soft embrace,
Gentle rhythms, a sacred space.
With each step, a heartbeat's flow,
In every heart, the will to grow.

Amidst the chaos, beauty wakes,
In unity, the earth partakes.
Together, hands and hearts align,
Crafting dreams in a world divine.

As petals fall, the music swells,
In whispers, nature's language dwells.
Euphony that stirs the soul,
Together, we become whole.

The Day Begins Anew

Morning breaks with a gentle glow,
Promises of warmth in soft winds blow.
Birdsong fills the air with cheer,
A brand new day is finally here.

Sunlight spills on dewy grass,
Time for dreams to gently pass.
The world awakens with a yawn,
Shimmering jewels of the dawn.

Each ray a brush of golden hue,
Painting skies in vibrant blue.
With every heartbeat, hope ignites,
Guiding us to new heights.

Paths unfold with endless grace,
Journeys start, we find our place.
In this moment, life unfolds,
In every story, love is told.

Embrace the dawn with open eyes,
Breathe in joy, let worries fly.
The day begins, a canvas wide,
With every brushstroke, dreams abide.

Cascading Joy

A river flows with laughter bright,
Each ripple dances in the light.
Joy cascades like waterfalls,
In every corner, beauty calls.

The sun winks down from azure skies,
Whispers of joy in nature's sighs.
Petals swirl in twirling air,
Fragments of joy, floating fair.

Children's laughter fills the streets,
In every heart, the rhythm beats.
Life's a song, a joyous blend,
Cascading love, we gladly send.

Moments shared, a smile exchanged,
In little things, our hearts are changed.
Through our days, let joy take hold,
A treasure more precious than gold.

As evening falls and stars ignite,
Cascading joy shines through the night.
In every whisper, every glance,
Life's an endless, joyful dance.

A Chronicle of Clarity

In the stillness, thoughts do flow,
Reflecting truths we yearn to know.
Like crystal waters, pure and bright,
They guide us softly through the night.

Each moment cherished, clear and bold,
In hearts of dreamers, stories unfold.
The path illuminated, step by step,
A journey woven, secrets kept.

Together we chase the dawn's embrace,
In the quiet, we find our place.
Voices echo, gentle and true,
In the light, we begin anew.

Whispers of wisdom fill the air,
Bringing solace, a tranquil prayer.
In clarity's embrace, we reside,
A tapestry of love and pride.

With every heartbeat, echoes resound,
In clarity's arms, we are found.
Hand in hand, together we stand,
A chronicle written in the sand.

Where Shadows Meet the Light

In the twilight where secrets lie,
Where whispers hum and shadows sigh.
The dance of day and night we see,
A fragile balance, wild and free.

Figures drift in the fading glow,
Past and future intertwine, flow.
Hints of laughter, echoes of strife,
Sketching out the canvas of life.

Where shadows deepen, hope ignites,
Stars awaken in starry nights.
Glimmers of dreams in darkened hues,
In this space, we start to choose.

A bridge of light born from the dark,
Fostering beauty, igniting spark.
Here in pausing breaths, we find,
The dance of time, forever entwined.

With every flicker, tales unfold,
Mingling silver with threads of gold.
Where shadows meet, we're drawn to light,
In the twilight, our spirits take flight.

Dawning upon a glistening Horizon

As dawn breaks with a gentle yawn,
Colors spill on the velvet lawn.
Soft whispers lift the night's retreat,
In stillness, magic feels complete.

Golden rays stretch wide and far,
Embracing dreams, like a guiding star.
Each sparkling dew, a precious token,
Of promises made and words unspoken.

Where sky meets sea in a warm embrace,
Nature's canvas, a wondrous space.
Mountains rise up, majestic and grand,
Crafted carefully by nature's hand.

In this dawn, we take our stand,
Awakening hearts and holding hands.
With every breath, we seize the day,
As hopes arise and shadows sway.

A horizon kissed by the sun's first light,
Inviting souls to take their flight.
Together we journey, side by side,
Towards the promise of what's inside.

A Quiet Revolution of Color

In the silence, hues collide,
Bursting forth, they gently glide.
Brushstrokes bold in twilight's hand,
A quiet revolution across the land.

Whispers of green in emerald fields,
Nature's palette, love reveals.
With every shade, a story told,
Of dreams ignited, hearts made bold.

Blues cascade like tranquil streams,
Awakening all the hidden dreams.
Each color shines with vibrant might,
Illuminating the darkest night.

Reds ignite a fierce desire,
A burning flame, a passionate fire.
In this canvas rich and vast,
The future glimmers, shadows cast.

Together we paint with strokes unique,
Finding beauty in every peak.
In this quiet revolution, we see,
The power of color sets us free.

Raindrops on Windows

Raindrops tap on glassy panes,
Whispers of the softest rains.
Nature's tears gently fall,
A soothing song, a tender call.

Each droplet tells a fleeting tale,
Of skies that danced with winds so frail.
They glide and race in sweet delight,
A ballet in the dusky light.

Patterns form and slowly fade,
Memories in the quiet made.
The world outside just fades away,
As I watch the raindrops play.

In every splash, a moment's peace,
A chance for all my thoughts to cease.
The rhythm calms my busy mind,
In droplets, solace I do find.

So I sit and close my eyes,
Listening to their softest sighs.
Raindrops dance, the world anew,
In this moment, just me and you.

Love Letters

In quiet ink, our words unwind,
Secrets whispered, hearts aligned.
Every curve ignites a spark,
A page echoes love's sweet mark.

With folded edges, dreams take flight,
Underneath the soft moonlight.
Promises wrapped in heartfelt lines,
A treasure chest of love divine.

Through the years these letters stay,
Chronicles of love's ballet.
Each ink drop holds a memory,
Of laughter shared, of ecstasy.

Addressed to you, my heart's own song,
In your embrace is where I belong.
Through every heartbeat, tender grace,
My love, my letters, time can't erase.

So write me still, let love inspire,
Each syllable, a burning fire.
Together we'll craft tales untold,
In love letters, our hearts unfold.

Fleeting Moments of Elation

A butterfly flits on the breeze,
Moments dance, intentions tease.
Laughter blooms in bursts of light,
Fleeting joy, a pure delight.

The sun dips low, the sky ablaze,
In twilight's grace, we lose our ways.
With each heartbeat, wishes soar,
Embracing life, wanting more.

A child's giggle, a lover's gaze,
These fleeting moments, a dazzling maze.
Time skips lightly, all aglow,
Like fireflies in evening's show.

Clouds may gather, storms might brew,
Yet in the chaos, love shines through.
Each fleeting smile, a sacred gift,
In these brief times, our spirits lift.

So hold these moments, let them stay,
In your heart, where dreams replay.
For fleeting joy, though brief and rare,
Becomes the magic that we share.

When Clouds Part to Shine

Gray skies linger, shadows creep,
The world beneath, a hush, a sleep.
Yet moments wait, the light's embrace,
As clouds part ways, revealing grace.

Sunbeams dance on dew-kissed grass,
Golden rays that softly pass.
A glimmer of hope, a warm caress,
Nature's beauty, our hearts confess.

In every crack, in every seam,
A miracle waits, a whispering dream.
When darkness blooms, we hold our breath,
For light returns, defying death.

So take a moment, breathe it in,
The burst of joy, where dreams begin.
Courage finds us, in shadows cast,
When clouds grow thin, our spirits last.

Each ray a promise, a life anew,
In every shadow, the light shines through.
When clouds part ways, we rise and shine,
With open hearts, like stars align.

The Undercurrent of Renewal

In silent depths, the waters flow,
With gentle whispers, secrets grow.
Beneath the surface, life abounds,
An undercurrent that astounds.

The ebb and flow, a dance of days,
Each cycle brings a new-found praise.
In stillness, we find the heart's sweet song,
As tides of time pull us along.

Renewal waits, a patient grace,
In every storm, we find our place.
With every trial, we rise anew,
An undercurrent, strong and true.

From ashes rise, like phoenix flight,
In darkest times, we seek the light.
Embracing change, we learn to grow,
Through life's rich tapestry, we flow.

So trust the waves, let's take the leap,
For in surrender, harvests reap.
The undercurrent calls us near,
A melody of joy, loud and clear.

Whispers of the Wet Earth

After the storm, the ground breathes,
Soft murmurs of life in the sod,
Nature shakes off the thunder's grip,
In droplets, the message of God.

Leaves glisten under the pale dawn,
Each petal adorned with fresh grace,
The earth sings in quiet tones,
As freshness paints every space.

A snail moves slow, tracing paths,
On a canvas of dampened soil,
With every inch, a story told,
In harmony, the world tends to toil.

Breezes weave through the tall grass,
Carrying scents of the new day,
Hovering like whispers of dreams,
Inviting all to come and play.

In the puddle, reflections dance,
Ripples break the solemn calm,
A fleeting glimpse of sky's deep hue,
Nature's tender, silent psalm.

Sunlight's Return

Morning breaks, a golden hue,
Fingers of light stretch and reach,
Chasing shadows from their dark,
Each ray, like a soft-spoken speech.

Birds awaken, stirring the air,
Their songs blend with the sun's rise,
A symphony of warm delight,
As light spills forth from the skies.

Warmed earth blooms beneath the glow,
Colors bursting, a visual feast,
The world rejoices in the warmth,
A celebration, to say the least.

Kites dance high on playful winds,
Children laugh with joy intertwined,
Sunlight wraps them in its glow,
Happy moments, sweet memories designed.

As dusk approaches, colors fade,
The sun bows low, a soft retreat,
Yet every sunset holds a promise,
Of tomorrow's warmth, a love so sweet.

Puddles of Reflection

Beneath the grey, the world lies still,
In puddles, secrets gently stir,
Mirrors of moments captured tight,
Of skies and dreams, of him and her.

With each drop, a tale unfolds,
Of laughter shared and tears that flow,
The pavement glimmers with their hopes,
In shimmering circles, stories glow.

Boots splash through, with carefree joy,
Rippling dreams beneath their feet,
Every footprint leaves a mark,
On chapters where memories greet.

Gazing down, the soul takes flight,
In those reflections, we can see,
The essence of the life we live,
And all the paths that set us free.

The rain may fall, but hearts stay warm,
In puddles, we find our truth, our home,
Each ripple a whisper of the past,
In still waters, we continue to roam.

The Blooming Encore

As winter fades, a curtain lifts,
A stage adorned with colors bright,
Petals unfold, a grand debut,
In gardens warmed by golden light.

Each flower sways, a gentle dance,
In rhythm with the soft spring breeze,
Their fragrant essence fills the air,
A tapestry of blooms with ease.

Nature calls, a wondrous show,
In every corner, life awakens,
From buds to blossoms, beauty grows,
The earth's sweet verse, deeply taken.

Honeybees hum their busy tune,
While butterflies kiss the day's embrace,
In this encore, life's perfect notes,
A celebration of vibrant grace.

As twilight falls, the colors fade,
But dreams of spring linger on,
In every heart a seed is sown,
For with each cycle, we are reborn.

Petals Glimmer Like Stars

Petals fall in gentle breeze,
Their shimmer catches moonlit seas.
In the garden, dreams take flight,
Whispered secrets in the night.

Colors dance, a fragrant tune,
Beneath the gaze of silver moon.
Each bloom tells a tale so bright,
In the shadows, love ignites.

Nature's brush paints soft and rare,
A tapestry beyond compare.
In every petal, hope does nest,
Cocooned in beauty, hearts find rest.

Time slows down in fragrant air,
As whispers weave without a care.
Each moment wrapped in soft delight,
Petals glimmer, pure and light.

Underneath a velvet sky,
Wishes float and softly fly.
Hands entwined, we share this hour,
In the garden's sacred power.

Shiny Roads to Tomorrow

Shiny roads stretch far and wide,
Promises twinkling, side by side.
With each step, a tale unfolds,
Adventures waiting, bright and bold.

Golden rays light up the way,
Guiding hearts through night and day.
In each corner, dreams align,
Paths converging, yours and mine.

Footprints dance on gravel's song,
Together, we are brave and strong.
With every turn, the future's near,
A journey blessed, we have no fear.

Endless horizons call our name,
In the distance, flickers of flame.
Hope ignites, a soft embrace,
Shiny roads, our dreams we chase.

Let's build a world of love and light,
Where shadows fade, and hearts take flight.
Together, we shall forge our way,
On shiny roads, come what may.

Misty Hues of Promise

Misty hues awaken dawn,
Veils of fog, a magic drawn.
In whispers, nature speaks to me,
With hidden wonders yet to see.

Softly wrapped in morning's glow,
Where dreams and reality flow.
Each moment holds a promise rare,
In the silence, love's declared.

Shadows dance on dew-kissed grass,
Painting scenes that gently pass.
In every glimmer, hope does twine,
Within the mist, our hearts align.

Through the veil, new worlds await,
Each breath a chance to navigate.
With courage sewn in every seam,
Misty hues awaken the dream.

Step by step, we'll find our way,
In the dawn of a brand new day.
With open hearts and spirits free,
Misty hues lead you to me.

Colors Reawakened

Colors burst in vibrant cheer,
Painting life in shades so dear.
From the canvas of the soul,
Artistry makes the spirit whole.

In every stroke, a story flows,
The heart's palette softly glows.
Through shadows bright and darkness deep,
Awakens dreams that never sleep.

Blues of calm and reds of fire,
Dancing notes in sweet desire.
Greens of life, a healing balm,
Colors weave a gentle calm.

Through stormy skies and sunny rays,
Each hue within our spirits plays.
In every moment, bright and true,
Colors reawaken, me and you.

Let's celebrate this vivid night,
With laughter echoing in flight.
In this canvas, love will stay,
Colors reawaken every day.

A Dance of Sunlight and Mist

In the early light, soft and bright,
Sunlight kisses the dew so light.
Misty veils drift and sway,
As day breaks, night fades away.

Whispers of dawn weave their charm,
Gentle breezes sing so warm.
Nature's canvas, hues unfold,
A dance of stories yet untold.

Golden rays through branches tease,
Creeping shadows, swaying trees.
Each breath of air, sweet delight,
In this moment, pure and right.

Colors merge in vibrant play,
As the morning greets the day.
Sun and mist, a fleeting kiss,
In nature's gentle, tender bliss.

Time stands still in this soft haven,
Where earth and sky are beautifully woven.
In every bead of dew, a spark,
Awakening life from the dark.

Treading Through Eau de Vie

Footsteps echo on cobblestone,
Each path tells tales, all alone.
The air is thick with scents divine,
Whispers of grapes on the vine.

A twilight glow, the world feels near,
Laughter and love, all so clear.
In glasses clink, stories unfold,
Liquid gold, memories retold.

The river flows, a song so sweet,
With every sip, life feels complete.
The dance of flavors, rich and bold,
In every moment, stories told.

Stars ignite in the velvet sky,
As dreams awaken and hearts fly.
With friends beside, the night a glow,
Treading softly on paths we know.

In this embrace, time drips slowly,
Each heartbeat lingers, ever so holy.
Together we breathe in the night,
Treading through eau de vie, pure delight.

Trembling Flowers in the Sun

Petals open to the warm embrace,
Sunlight dances on every trace.
Colors burst, a vivid show,
As gentle breezes start to blow.

Beneath the sky, a lively sweep,
Nature's secrets softly creep.
In the garden, magic thrives,
Where trembling flowers come alive.

Each bloom a heartbeat, bold and bright,
A tapestry of pure delight.
In every hue, a story spun,
Whispering softly, all is one.

Butterflies flit with playful grace,
In the sun's warm, glowing space.
Nature's laughter fills the air,
In this realm, beauty is rare.

The world awakens, a vibrant sight,
With trembling flowers, hearts take flight.
In each blossom, life's sweet plea,
To embrace the now, wild and free.

Nature's Breathe of Liberation

In every rustle, a gentle sigh,
Nature breathes, as time slips by.
Mountains rise, whispering tall,
In their shadows, we find it all.

Rivers flow with stories untold,
Carving paths through the earth so bold.
Each wave a voice in the endless sea,
Calling softly to you and me.

Leaves flutter like whispers of dreams,
In the sunlight, the world gleams.
The air, a chorus rich and deep,
Awakening wonders from their sleep.

In every breeze, a promise made,
Life's simple joys beautifully displayed.
In solitude, we find our way,
Nature's breath guides us each day.

With every heartbeat, we connect,
In the wild, we reflect and protect.
In the dance of life, we discover,
Nature's breath, our endless lover.

Unfurled Leaves in the Sun

New buds awaken in the morn,
Softly kissed by light reborn.
Whispers dance upon the trees,
In the glow, a gentle tease.

Shadows play on emerald ground,
Nature's beauty all around.
With every hue, the world ignites,
In the sun, pure joy delights.

Branches sway, a joyful tune,
Underneath the vibrant moon.
Calmly swaying, hearts released,
In this warmth, all worries ceased.

Through the canopies, light weaves,
Painting dreams on curling leaves.
Unfurled wonders, life anew,
In the sun's embrace, we grew.

Time stands still in nature's clutch,
Every moment feels the touch.
With open hearts, we breathe it in,
Unfurled leaves, let life begin.

A Canvas Awash with Light

Colors burst across the sky,
A masterpiece that catches eye.
Brushstrokes bold and vivid shine,
Each hue crafted, so divine.

Clouds stretch wide like gentle hands,
Bringing beauty to the lands.
Sunset whispers of the day,
In a blaze, it fades away.

Morning breaks, a canvas fresh,
With the dawn, all colors mesh.
Gold and blue and softest gray,
A new art piece born each day.

As the stars begin to glow,
Night unveils its quiet show.
In the dark, the light glints bright,
A canvas awash with pure delight.

Every shade tells tales untold,
In warm sunlight, the world unfolds.
With each sunrise, dreams take flight,
In the stillness, hearts unite.

Tenderness Lingers in the Breeze

Gentle whispers through the air,
Nature's soft and loving care.
Petals flutter, hearts do sway,
In the breeze, they drift away.

Sunlight glows on fields of green,
A quiet grace, a soothing scene.
Moments cherished, time stands still,
In this warmth, we feel the thrill.

Echoed laughter through the trees,
Dance of shadows, softest tease.
With every breath, the world ignites,
In the beauty, pure delight.

Holding hands, a fleeting touch,
In the breeze, we find so much.
Every heartbeat, every sigh,
Tenderness that cannot die.

Whispers linger, hearts entwined,
In this moment, love defined.
Through the meadow, dreams unfurl,
Tenderness, our precious pearl.

The Dancer's Embrace with Moisture

Raindrops twirl on wooden floors,
Nature's rhythm softly pours.
In the light, a glimmer plays,
The dancer's heart begins to sway.

Wet earth sings beneath her feet,
Every step, a gentle beat.
With arms outstretched to the gray,
She finds joy within the spray.

Melodies of water fall,
Whispered secrets in her thrall.
Every movement, grace defined,
Moisture wraps her, pure, aligned.

Through the storm, she leaps and spins,
With each twirl, a new life begins.
Lost in moments, wild and free,
A symphony of harmony.

So she dances, free and bold,
Embracing warmth from drops of cold.
In the rain, her spirit gleams,
The dancer's embrace fuels her dreams.

Milton Keynes UK
Ingram Content Group UK Ltd.
UKHW022224251124
451566UK00006B/109